Arctic Queen

Magic of the Everyday

Arctic Queen

Magic of the Everyday

A poetic story about mindfulness

Dignity Press
World Dignity University Press

Arctic Queen (www.arctic-queen.com) is the pseudonym of Ragnhild Nilsen, one of Scandinavia`s greatest public speakers and inspirators. Besides being a gifted storyteller, singer and composer, she is the author of 14 books – both poetic novels and more practical books about leadership, presentation skills and change management.

Arctic Queen spends much of her time on the ecological cotton revolution, an initiative she has taken together with SEKEM on behalf of global warming and fair trade. See www.globalfairtrade.com and www.sekemscandinavia .com.

Published October 2014 by:
Dignity Press
16 Northview Court
Lake Oswego, OR 97035, USA
www.dignitypress.org/magic-everyday

Printed on paper from environmentally managed forestry:
http://www.lightningsource.com/chainofcustody

ISBN 978-1-937570-53-8

Dedicated to Anne Katrine

It happened one beautiful summer morning. The sun sent its rays across the landscape and roused it from its nocturnal slumber. The dew lay like tiny beads of crystal upon the grass, and an army of ants had begun their day's work. A crow pulled a worm from the black, soft soil, while the beautiful song of a thrush rang out from a tree right above. The countless colours, smells and sounds revealed themselves in these first hours of the day, just as they do every single morning.

A brown butterfly with yellow stripes on its wings, fluttered across the meadow. It wanted to sip the nectar of some pink dog roses that coiled down a little slope. The butterfly was unaware of being observed by a girl who lay in the meadow and chewed upon a blade of grass. The girl's name was Eutychia. She thought this butterfly very beautiful – even though it didn't stand out in any obvious way from the other brown and yellow butterflies on the meadow this morning. She was just about to count them, when she noticed that the little butterfly she had laid eyes on, had come too close to one of the dog roses' thorns and now its wing was stuck.

Eutychia raised herself quickly up and ran across to the slope with the roses. She reached out her hand and carefully lifted the delicate butterfly away from the thorn. It remained upon her fingertips for a few moments before it took off into the air. The damage to the wing was not so great as to prevent it from flying on. The girl smiled with joy. She gazed upon the rapid beat of the butterfly's tiny wings as they carried it in an arc around and over the rosebush.

At that very moment something rather strange happened. A golden glow came over the tiny form of the butterfly. Its wings and body began to grow and behind the antennae she saw there hid a tiny, cheery little face. On this particular morning, which resembled any other morning, a butterfly turned into a fairy.

–It's happened. Finally it's happened! I've become a fairy!

Eutychia strained to listen. Where had that delightful, melodious voice come from?

– I felt the pain of the thorn and thought I was about to die and then something magical happened.

– You can speak? Eutychia exclaimed in astonishment.

The fairy nodded its tiny head.

– All my life I've wanted to be a fairy, you see. And now, when I least expected it, the miracle occurred!

The delightful little figure landed on Eutychia's shoulder. She looked down upon it and smiled in wonder. Eagerly it continued:

– Since you have saved my life, little girl, I will grant you one wish. What is it that you wish for most in your life?

– I don't know…

– What kind of answer is that?

The fairy took off from her shoulder and flew around to hover in the air in front of her face. Eutychia could not help but notice how the butterfly became visibly more and more beautiful. The entirety of its little form glowed now as it danced in front of her like a golden orb.

– Before something magical can happen, you need to wish for it, said the fairy eagerly.

– But I haven't had time to think about what I want to wish for yet, protested Eutychia.

– When the time is here, it is here, said the little fairy in a decisive tone.

– Dare to believe in your dreams!

Eutychia gazed for a while at some sheep that grazed peacefully across the meadow, oblivious to the extraordinary event taking place in front of the rosebush. Finally she squeezed her eyes shut, summoned up her courage and in a firm and clear voice said:

– Dear fairy. I wish that the joy I felt when I rescued you from the thorn will stay with me for the rest of my life.

– Ooh. That's a lot to wish for, said the fairy and danced further up into the air.

A sprinkling of some kind of light dust fell down upon the girl's long brown hair. Some of the other butterflies crept out of their nectar pockets in order to take a peek at this beautiful sparkling shower.

The fairy flew over to Eutychia and right up to her ear. It whispered some words to her that she alone could hear. Then it fluttered elegantly over the rosebush and flew further out over the meadow to the other side which faced the woods. Eutychia followed the fairy with her eyes until it was no bigger than a little dot on the edge of the woods. Then it was gone.

The yellow and brown butterflies disappeared back to their search for nectar. The crow found a new worm which it gobbled up, and the ants continued their work with the anthill. Eutychia never saw the fairy again. Yes, there were days when she wondered if she had really met a fairy, or whether it had simply been a product of her imagination – a childish fantasy.

What Eutychia came to see was her everyday life. Days came towards her, one by one, year after year – with their attendant events, experiences and feelings. She met sorrow and hardship. She ran into different kinds of disappointments and anxiety. She was tested by ordeals and defeats. But no one could take her inner joy away. She kept it in her heart like a tiny butterfly.

In time Eutychia grew older. It was whispered that she harbored a deep secret. Some people told how their own dissatisfaction and insecurity paled in her presence, and that they were reminded of the best and most beautiful moments of their lives when they were together with her. Others said she inspired them to do good deeds. They felt like doing more, daring more and making more use of their talents when they spoke to her.

Whenever anyone asked what her magic was however, she would smile and answer bashfully.

– I met a fairy when I was a little girl. It whispered some words in my ear.

And if they wanted to know what the fairy had said, she told them:

– That which a fairy whispers in your ear, should not be divulged.

Every day came and went. Eutychia grew to become an old woman. One morning she lay sick in bed and knew that she had to prepare herself for the final journey into the everlasting. When they heard this, people flocked to her bedside. Some to say: "If it hadn't been for your joy, I would not have found mine!" Others to remind her of some tenderness she had displayed, a conversation held, a friendly word spoken unexpectedly, a confidence shown when others doubted, a promise held, an insight given in the right moment.

The old woman was overwhelmed by people's heartfelt warmth, and the stories they told about how her life had given them faith and hope. She was astonished that she had meant so much to so many without herself knowing it.

While everyone stood by the bed to say their goodbyes, one of them, whom she knew well, came with a request:

– Eutychia, he said.

– You can't leave us without revealing the secret. What was it the fairy told you at the time you were a little girl?

An expression of inner certainty spread across the old woman's face.

– Yes. I shall tell you. Now the time is right. But since I have no children of my own, let me look into the face of a young girl. I will reveal to her my secret.

Thus it came to pass that I met the old woman Eutychia. She took my hand and looked into my eyes. I heard her gentle voice, full of days, and heavy with the weight of experience, talk to me.

– When I was a little girl like you, I met a fairy in a meadow one beautiful summer morning. The fairy whispered to me: "If you want joy in your life, start every day by giving thanks. And when you fall asleep, count your blessings instead of sheep."

Eutychia gave a slight smile and closed her eyes while she continued.

– Know this. The source of joy lies hidden within the gift of gratitude, my child!

After the old woman had uttered these words, it was quiet for a good while. I glanced up at the people gathered around the bed, and I could see that they were pondering what they had just heard.

The old woman bade me come closer. I leaned over to her.

– Look under my pillow, she whispered. I let my hand slide under the large, white, lace-trimmed pillow until I felt my fingertips touch something. I withdrew my arm and looked down. In my hand I held a pile of yellowed hand-written sheets of paper wrapped up in a ribbon of golden silk.

- My beloved husband gave me these ancient letters and prescriptions just before his death a year ago, she said.
- He was a professor and archaeologist. These secret texts came into his possession through bizarre circumstances from an antique dealer in Egypt. He claimed that the letters were part of the extraordinary find made by an Egyptian farmer near the town of Nag Hammadi in the winter of 1945. These secret writings were probably concealed within the clay pot by a Coptic monk around 300 AD. The original scroll now lies hidden at the Jung Institute in Zurich. The old woman sighed before she continued.
- As my husband translated and deciphered the scroll, he found that it contained letters and prescriptions written by a Greek doctor named Theophilus, to a woman by the same name as myself.

She smiled quietly. I nodded and asked her to continue: Perhaps she was a scholar or maybe just a figment of the doctor's imagination. It was not unheard of, at that time, for scholars to write letters with a certain ethical or moral message to a fictional character, instead of writing a textbook. A Greek physician of the time would also have a full command of Latin, which was the official language. For the sake of curiosity, my husband has left some of the Latin words remain in the translated text.

Her eyes had a twinkle in them as she looked up at me.

– Now these ancient letters are yours. Open them and read them when you need to find hidden paths to your inner joy.

She smiled kindly, but indicated to all of us that she was tired and wanted to rest.

The old woman died the same night as I began to read the Greek doctor Theophilus' letters to Eutychia – friend of joy. Since then I have had the pleasure of reading them many times, and now you may too.

The Magic of the Everyday

is not to travel far away,

but to find your way home.

Letter One

Honourable Eutychia,

Such self-deception it is to believe that one finds oneself by travel. We can travel here and there, but now and again these journeys call forth two importunate questions: What are we travelling away from? And what are we travelling towards?

I myself have been afraid to settle down. Perhaps that is why I have not started a family. I've longed to be free, to be able to travel where I want, when I want and always have the time to do whatever suits me. Lately however – and perhaps this is because I have felt compelled to reside in one place for a while now – I do miss a home and a woman I can call my own. I don't think this need for a home is merely a matter of me looking for a permanent place of residence. Family, wedlock, a domicile, shared memories – all this gives a person the shelter he or she needs. What I long for is the feeling of belonging. Maybe I should dare to say it right out: I long to love, and to be loved in return.

I have been in love, several times during the festivals of Artemis. But the greatest amore I've ever experienced was while I studied to become a physician in Athens. My father had travelled back to my hometown Antioch, and I remained behind to absorb myself in medicine.

One night I visited a brothel. I was more than a little nervous of women, and decided to plunge into the adventure that had occupied my feverish fantasy for so long. However, Bacchus failed to lift my soul. Bashful and unsure of myself, I sought to steal further away from the noise and erotic shrieks of delight in the main room. I remember that I blushed as I stumbled into an ebullient companion of mine. His laughter made me even more ill at ease. Eventually, I realized that I had to throw up and I emptied the contents of my stomach in the garden outside the kitchen. When I had dried the cold sweat from my brow, I caught sight of a girl in the light from the kitchen door. I had never seen a more beautiful sight. A goddess with long, golden hair standing there, chopping onions. Was she a slave? I remained standing, and stared – for a long time. Then the girl glanced up, and I looked into those cheery sky-blue eyes for the first time. It was only then I noticed that I was cold and shivering. But I wanted to meet her and find out who she was. Fortune smiled upon me. At the gable end of the house there was a door that led right into the kitchen. I tried to open it quietly but it screeched like a hungry cat. A heavyset man turned around to face me:

"And how may I help the young gentlemen? This is no place for guests of the house."

I wanted to lie. I wanted to say I had taken a wrong turn, but I couldn't manage to say anything at all.

"The young gentleman smells of vomit," continued the well-built fellow, who was probably the cook. "You can avail of the bathroom outside to wash yourself."

At that moment the blue eyes looked at me and I remember that I thought: 'How can eyes that are so light blue be so deep?' They were like an ocean you could throw yourself into.

The girl laughed at me, or with me. I wasn't sure which. I wanted to bolt for the door, but I changed my mind and stammered:

"My apologies."

"That's quite all right," said the cook.

I summoned up all my courage.

"Who is she?"

The bulky fellow shook his head: "She is the owner's daughter and is not for sale."

The very next morning I was back again. The house was asleep, closed up and locked. I sneaked along the outer wall until I found a place where I could climb over. I remember that when I jumped down on the other side, I landed in some sharp and prickly rosebushes. I remained sitting while I prayed in earnest to Venus, the goddess of love. And she heard my prayers, because coming right towards me across the grass was the girl from the night before. I was nearly afraid to breathe, but my heart pounded so hard that I was sure she heard it. She may well have done, because she suddenly gave a start and stared right at me.

"It's only me," I said.

"I can see that," she said and smiled. "What are you doing here?"

"I'm looking for a girl with golden hair."

I tried to appear casual, but I must have looked like a wild cat with its hackles raised as I crept out from under the bush.

That was the beginning of a wonderful, but all too brief summer. Nearly every afternoon for an entire month, we were under Aphrodite's protection and found cunning places to rendezvous where we could kiss each other until we lost our senses. Sometimes we fell asleep in each other's arms. Sometimes we conversed upon thoughts that occupied our minds.

One afternoon she failed to turn up at the place where we had agreed to meet. I thought she was ill, but after a few days, where I waited for my love and she still hadn't turned up, I understood that which I did not want to know: She and her father had left for Ephesus. Her family did not want us to have any more contact. The acknowledgement of this fact felt like a spear had pierced my heart. Blood gushed forth. The pain was so strong that I could hardly breathe.

Days and weeks went by. I was unable to talk to anyone of my heartache. After some time, I threw myself into my medical studies with excessive zeal.

When I read through what I have written, I cannot help but think: 'Alas, Theophilus. You are lonely now!' But I, who am all too well acquainted with the icy claw of loneliness, know how to value the warming hearth of fellowship. It serves to console me, living like a stranger while I wait for word of what will happen to my friend, Paul the Apostle.

Honourable Eutychia. This is now my second winter in Rome. I have learnt the names of the mighty aqueducts, the bowed arches that throw themselves down the mountain with leaps and bounds in chained rows of water. They are magnificent constructions, but they hide no secrets nor sing any songs of praise unto God. They serve the concrete in the everyday life of the people.

Sometimes it snows here. Not so much as to turn the city white, but still enough for me to gather up a handful and watch it dissolve in the warmth of my palm. Ice forms around the shutters of my room and I am so cold at night that I have difficulty sleeping. The landlady brings me extra blankets. When I complain that I'm still freezing, she laughs at me and says that I'm not much of a doctor if I can't conjure up some warmth for myself. I recently took her advice to heart and bought myself a large fur lined cloak. I place a sprig of thyme in the pocket of the cloak to draw strength. But what is a meagre herb that's ruled by Venus compared to a beautiful, living, breathing woman? Perhaps I should try smelling a sprig of oregano, so that Aphrodite may transform me the way she transformed the favourite in Cyprus. My Grandmother introduced me to the legend when I was still a child:

"A long, long time ago," she said, "the island of Cyprus was ruled by the mighty King Cinyras. He had splendid palaces and gardens where the most fragrant flowers and herbs grew. Every summer, they were gathered by carefully selected and beautiful virgins who made precious perfumes from the plants. Well-known artists made ornate jars to preserve the scents in. Aphrodite visited the King every year, and every year she received a wonderful gift – a jar filled with exquisite perfume.

One morning while she was visiting the King, her gift was being carried over to her by a favourite who managed to drop the jar to the floor and break it. The valuable perfume ran out. The favourite was beside himself with shame and fear and promptly fainted. The King, who was wild with rage, was about to kill the young boy with his sword where he lay on the floor between fragrance and shards of the jar. The goddess Aphrodite however, stood in front of the boy and protected him. When she stepped aside, the favourite had been transformed into a fragrant red origanum vulgare. She picked up the plant carefully in her hands and glided up through the air to Olympus. She planted the oregano in a mountain crevice to the delight of all and sundry. Never again did she return to the King.

Honourable Eutychia. I say that I have felt compelled to be here in Rome. This is an exaggeration. No one has compelled me to do anything, least of all Paul. He is my friend, and has perhaps been my closest confidante in recent years. We became acquainted in the strangest of circumstances. I was aboard a ship sailing from Alexandria to Rome. There were several hundred people on board. I noticed in particular a Roman officer who had some soldiers and a number of prisoners travelling with him. For several days we lolled along with little wind, but when we reached the coast of Crete a severe storm caught up with us. The ship was swept along. It proved impossible to fight the wind, so we gave up and allowed ourselves to drift. The bad weather continued for several days. We had no idea where we were. Then I caught sight of the Roman officer together with the captain and one of the prisoners, a small stooped man who radiated an extreme power. I overheard the prisoner say: "People have gone without food for too long now. Give us something to eat. It's necessary in order for everyone to be saved. Do not worry. No one on board the ship will have so much as a hair upon their head come to harm."

I thought it a peculiar speech. In the middle of the night the sailors finally made landfall. And when the food came, we were all heartened. I asked them to cook some extra sage for us, that healing herb that even the gods are given to eating and drinking.

The new day dawned but no one recognized the coastline. We saw a bay with a flat beach and it was here the captain wanted to try and run the ship aground. We drifted towards a sandbank surrounded by water. The bow dug in deeply and stood firm. Bit by bit the stern was broken into pieces by the surf. A few of the soldiers together with the Roman officer wanted to kill the prisoners in order to stop any possible attempts to swim to freedom, but the officer intervened. He gave orders that those who could swim should jump overboard and make their way to the beach. The others could follow on planks and other parts of the wreckage. Thus we all made it safely to land.

We gathered up twigs and lit a fire, as it was cold and raining. Suddenly a serpent crept out of the pile of twigs we had made and bit the prisoner who had predicted that we would all be saved. He shook the serpent off and cast it into the fire. I had no basil to extract the poison with, so I waited for him to swell up and die. "The man is probably a murderer," I thought, "since the gods don't see fit to allow him to live even though he survived the sea." But nothing unusual happened to him. I was astonished, and I ventured to ask the Roman officer from the Imperial Battalion who the prisoner was. He told me that the prisoner was called Paul and that some Jews in Jerusalem wanted to have him killed because he led a new religious movement. "He claims that it's possible to rise from the dead," said the officer and shook his head. "Paul is on the way to Rome to conduct his case in front of the Emperor."

Honourable Eutychia. I know the rhythm of Rome now and not just that which is created by the hours of the day and the changing of the seasons. There is another rhythm here. Powerful as the ebb and flow of the tides. It derives its strength from the tension of the population. The irritation increases from day to day. The quarrel lies just under the surface. The gossip is intense. Laughter tears up a conversation. The air vibrates. The cries become shriller. Quarrels explode into fistfights. One day when the tension borders the intolerable, the alleyways, the shops and the taverns empty. In countless numbers, the people flock to the games, where the gladiators redeem them in combat with lions or martyrs. One can hear the screams and cries from the arena for hours. And when the evening comes, the city breathes out. People find their way home. Cleansed. Tired. Liberated. The fountains are scented with lavender to mask the stench of blood.

Fortunately, Paul has still time to win his case. The winter lies for a while yet, like a skirt covering the arena. Personally I have my doubts. The Emperor Nero is one of those who transform the world to their own liking, with the particular strength that lack of sensitivity gives. Progress directed, yet myopic. Even though he buys shiploads of rose petals for gold, he is closed and without mercy. Will the Emperor listen to Paul's words about the mysteries of the heart? Or will he use the Apostle as carrion?

I must not lose hope. As a doctor, I know that hope is more than a naïve thought that everything will turn out alright in the end. Those of my patients who have hope, assure themselves and others all the time that they will reach their targets, even though things look difficult. They are humble enough to try out different ways.

Hope opens up the hearts of men, as the marigold flower opens itself to the sun. Perhaps that is why calendula officinalis is one of my favourite herbs. Its pale-yellow or orange edge crown tells me that it is of high rank in nature. Strained marigold cures all feverish ills and can be shaped into relieving ointments. It helps us to balance our mood and thus makes us laugh.

I remember a conversation I had with a patient who had developed a melancholic illness, because she worried too much about the transitory nature of life.

"Sooner or later it's over," she said pensively while she sipped the warm drink I gave her. "Nothing remains."

I attempted to get her to acknowledge that the transience of life does not diminish its meaning. I could not manage it at first, so I used a Socratic dialogue. I asked her if she had ever met a person whose efforts and achievements she respected. To my delight she answered that the old family doctor had been an exceptional person.

"Did he die?" I asked.

"Yes," she answered.

"But his life was meaningful, was it not?"

"If anyone's life has been meaningful, his must have been."

"Imagine now that not one single patient remembers what they owe this doctor, because people are ungrateful and quick to forget. Does his lifework endure then?"

"It endures," she mumbled.

"But when all his patients are dead, then what?"

"It endures that his life was meaningful," she said and smiled to me. Her melancholy was cured.

*H*onourable Eutychia. When you get up in the morning, make it a habit to say to yourself: I was lucky to wake up today. I am a living, breathing person. I will have friendly thoughts about others. I will use all my energy to grow in both wisdom and knowledge.

Then put a little rosemary in the water when you bathe yourself, or crush flowers and leaves and carry them in a canvas bag around your right arm. This will fill you with mirth and put a spring in your step.

It is easy to lose the ability to see things in perspective during your everyday. If your spouse or a friend withdraws for a week, you can begin to regard the distance as the truth about the whole relationship – instead of realizing that he or she is going through a difficult period and simply needs some breathing space. Instead of losing yourself in insecurity, try and see those close to you as independent individuals, who experience mood swings and patterns of response that don't necessarily have anything to do with you. Silence need not imply rejection.

Learn to leave other people alone sometimes – just leave them be, and let them sort out their lives themselves. In order to do that you need to rid yourself of the idea that you can change your partner or friend, and that it is within your power to put things right in the other person's life. You can only put things right in your own life. Your relationships with other people – whether good or bad – reflect your own strengths and weaknesses. If you can look at your relationships from this angle, you'll find it easier to forgive the people around you for their failings and put their blunders behind you. Remember this:

Hope comes with solutions that offer hope. Joy comes with participation.

People who contribute to solving problems are less depressed than those who stand and watch without doing anything. In this way, Paul is a master. I shall call him the Apostle of Hope. I have never seen him yield to overwhelming anxiety, defensive attitudes or depression. Even though he has, time and time again, been faced with the most difficult of challenges and setbacks.

Some time ago, I was at a tavern and I over-heard the story of his capture in the city of Philippi, which is an important town for the Romans in the province of Macedonia. He had been accused of stirring up trouble and causing riots there because he had healed a lame man and released a woman from an evil prophecy. After a severe beating, he was placed in the innermost dungeon with his feet in the block together with the worst criminals. At midnight he began to sing songs of praise to God. All of a sudden there was an earthquake so powerful that it shook the prison to its very foundations. All at once the doors burst open and all the chains fell off. The prison guard, who had fallen asleep, seized his sword and was about to take his own life, for he thought all the prisoners had escaped. With all his strength, Paul shouted out to him: "You must not harm yourself. We are all here."

The prison guard lit a torch, ran into the dun-geon and fell at Paul's feet. He nursed the prison-ers' wounds with yarrow ointment and the next day he took the apostle home to his own house, gave him food and drink and let him go.

Yes. Paul bears his destiny like a hero. He is my mother's ideal son in that respect.

onourable Eutychia. While I write this, I picture an episode from my life. It began with a letter I received from my Father. He wrote that my grandmother was beginning to grow very old. It was high time that I paid her a visit. Thus I went. After a few days sailing we reached the port outside Antioch. Grandmother lived on the banks of the Orontes, which provides the city with an abundance of clear, fresh water. I went up the narrow steps that wound between the terraces to the herb garden and noted with satisfaction that the spice plants had begun to bud as they should in the early spring warmth.

I leaned against a cypress tree, an unusual tree and a stranger like myself on this gentle slope opposite the house where I grew up. The branches could not conceal me, but I felt as safe as if I was in a clever hiding place.

The expansive landscape lay clear and cool in the early morning. I don't know what stirred me most – the naked clear swath from the mountain ridges, forests and fields in relief against a pearl pale sky – or the sound of goat bells under the olive trees. Maybe it was the light playing upon the horizon.

The mist was about to clear from the hollows and plains. The air was refreshingly cool with a weak hint of thyme and rosemary. The grass was moist with dew. The land was at rest within itself and it breathed of something timeless, that the language of men has not words for.

'The bonds that tie me to this place are mystical in nature,' I thought. 'Even if I should leave now, never to return again, the bonds would still hold me with their own peculiar strength. As long as some of my own flesh and blood are here, I too will have a home in this place.'

I caught sight of something, a bouquet of exquisite colour that could not be attributed to this shy spring morning. It was my Grandmother in person, dressed in a blue brocaded dressing gown. Obviously lost in thought, she came out and leaned against the garden wall. I watched from the distance. Between us the thin grey country road meandered lazily over the plain, up and down the hills, like a determined and persistent expression of human yearning and mankind's belief that it is better to be in one place instead of another.

"Life simulates," my father had written. "The old dear pretends. Imagination takes her away, like the sail of a small boat where the ballast has been thrown overboard. Now she nearly gets lost in her own bedroom. After Grandfather died, she has been left with a longing that does not belong to the past, but to the future. The servants and slaves marvel at the flaws in her memory. At the beginning, they thought it was the memories that faded. But no. For her, today is older than yesterday."

From where I stood, hidden behind the cypress tree, I tried to reconstruct the images of the Grandmother from my childhood. I longed to hear that voice which was so filled with the past, and I pictured a time long ago, when we walked hand in hand along the beach and she told me that the sea weeps in sympathy with all those that have lost a loved one.

I hurried across the road and called her name. The old woman lifted her head, squinted her eyes into small cracks and asked who I was. "Theophilus," I replied. She stretched out her hands and let her fingers run over my face. Then she touched me upon the lips. Finally she put her arms around my shoulders and said emphatically: "Theophilus. We shall have a warm day." At that moment, I remembered how my Grandmother had always proclaimed the most everyday events in tones of such solemn dignity. "Let us go into the house," she said. "And dear Theophilus, do me a favour. Call me Grandma. So I may still regard you as a child."

We went slowly towards the house. The sun hadn't quite risen above the horizon yet, but its hidden brilliance already gilded the top of the almond tree.

Ego sum vester tamquam famulus.

Theophilus

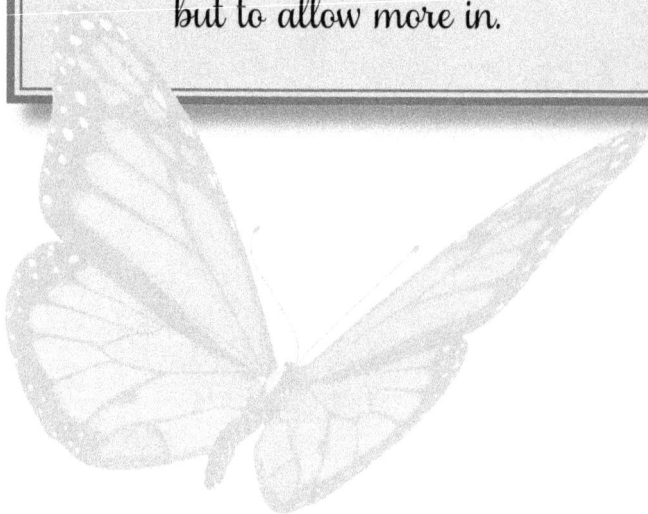

The Magic of the Everyday

is not to own more,

but to allow more in.

Letter Two

Honourable Eutychia,

On the first day of spring, in the sign of Pisces, accompanied by the birds that perched along the breadth of the slow flowing Orontes River, I was born into the world.

They named me Theophilus – friend of God.

I am, by nature, a man of contradiction. Arrogant. Constantly attracted to the supreme roles and the illustrious heroes. At the same time, I am prone to searching and unsure of my place in life. For several years, I have studied how this arrogance finds expression, and how offended I become when someone else threatens my role as the superior one. I have also discovered a coldness – a distance I can suddenly put between myself and a person who comes too close.

All through my life I have studied peoples' reactions, the hidden game that serves to protect them from offence. Mother was a good teacher. She was never angry, but she strove for perfection in art, in dance, in running a household, and in raising children. Perhaps that is why I remember her as chronically worried – because my imperfection was so plain to see. I was not a dream child by anyone's standards.

Four years after me, my sister came into the world. She was by nature a quiet child, displaying few obscure impulses or inclinations. I remember how impressed everyone was by her constant everyday happiness. If she was put to bed before the sun had gone down, she did not protest. Instead she lay in bed and sang. The same simple melody every night. Enveloped by her song, we sat in silence and watched the last rays of the sun fall across the earth.

I have another enduring image of my sister. She is standing in the fields, a little way off from where some friends and I have built a tree house. She's looking for me. I shout out for her to go home, but she remains standing. I shout out that she must go and find another place to play. But she doesn't go. Then I begin to throw stones at her. She remains standing there. Without crying. It is obvious that she's upset. She wants to be with me and she can't understand why her love is not reciprocated.

It was often like this. My own half-heartedness and pride prevented me from accepting that which she and others wanted to give me. Subsequently, I have come to think that this is a familiar pattern in many people's lives. We deny ourselves joy because it's seen as childish and naïve. We relinquish the nature of joy because we imagine that this will make us stronger. Instead we fill ourselves up with negative thoughts and worries.

When I was six, I could read and write. I received the same schooling as all Greek sons in Antioch – my father was Greek, my mother of Syrian descent – and I excelled at mathematics. My teacher believed that numbers were the key to the essence of everything, but his quest for absolute conceivability bored me after a time. At an early age I read Aristotle and was fascinated by his philosophy that man gains happiness through succeeding. "We are what we repeatedly do. Excellence then, is not an act, but a habit." Later I met the world of ideas in Plato's writings, and I agreed with him that happiness must be bound up with something more constant than the realization of personal talents. I perceived the truth in Socrates' words that nothing evil could befall the good.

My parents and grandparents were like most Greeks. We all took part in the annual festivals, and bore sacrifices to the gods. I remember Artemis, the beautiful virgin goddess, and the feasts to honour her in the springtime. Even now I can still admire the goddess with the innumerable breasts. Her body is swathed in all the creatures of the forests and the fields, not to mention the enormous bees – the very symbol of her fertility. The flames of the bonfires rose toward the sky and we shared the meat of the sacrificed lamb. The goddess filled the air with her presence and her gentle tenderness for ordinary mortals.

My mother wanted me to be strong and independently minded. I was to be of unblemished character with a mind of my own. The unclouded hero. I remember how quick she herself was to deny every bad feeling, so brutally in fact that she didn't acknowledge them. Until the unreleased emotions festered in her mind and came to cast a shadow over her entire existence.

I don't know how long Mother had been ill before we became aware of it. Perhaps the illness is the reason why I remember her as pallid and thin and rather serious. In the spring of my twelfth year, she couldn't manage to keep her food down and she was in great pain. When the old doctor came, he squeezed on my mother's stomach and shook his head. There was nothing anyone could do. Mother grew sicker every day, but she didn't want me or my sister around her. We didn't even have permission to visit her. I was happy in a way, because it meant I was now free to run wild in the forest with the dogs and with my friends. Many of them were the children of the house slaves. We climbed trees, scattered pigeons or tormented small chickens. Sometimes I played in the little pottery workshop where my grandmother made jars and bowls of clay, or I drew in the atelier that belonged to my father and grandfather. There was a multitude of people in that big house and always something to do.

One day Father told us that Mother was dying. Fate had deemed it so. I went out into the court-yard between the house and the wall that pro-tected us from intruders. A mighty almond tree grew here, that cast its shadow over the yard. I sat down on a bench under the tree. I felt the weight of sadness descend upon me. I sat there all afternoon and gazed at the Indian thrushes – as if trying to regain my strength with the help of the caged birds. It began to rain. My sister came and sat down quietly beside me. After a while she took my hand. The raindrops fell upon the leaves of the almond tree like my own small tear-filled gasps.

If my sister and I had grown up under the auspices of Mother, the hero ideal would most likely have taken shape strongly and clearly, and I would have remained a well-read and critical Greek. But after Mother's death, I was set adrift. My lust for life became a dried up river. No wind filled the sail of my dreams. When the almond tree outside the window opened into clusters of pink blossoms, my melancholy grew into despair. Because a young man could not find the meaning of life? Or because the yearning of the soul was unbearable?

Father brought me along to the temples. We offered up sacrifices to Zeus and Athena, Apollo and Artemis. One of the priests bid my father boil hyssop in wine and give it to me to drink morning and evening. "Jupiter's plant will cure the boy," he said. But the gods did not listen to our prayers. I dragged myself along the road like a sick dog. The landscape I passed was dashed with despondency. Spring stuck to my eyes.

Grandmother began to become worried about me and gave me plenty of parsley to eat – petroselinum foliosum crispum. She consoled me with the tale of the hero Archemorus who was wounded on the island of Istmos. "Parsley grew for the very first time upon the patch of earth where the drops of his blood fell," she said. "The herb gave him his strength back." Grandmother always framed our herb garden with a border of parsley, as is the custom. She also weaved the fresh green herb into festive garlands at different feast times.

The priest at the temple gave me strained borage to drink. "This will give you back your will to live," he said. The plant grows in the sign of Leo, and perhaps it was that savoury herb that gave my heart a yearning to make something of my life. It was, as I recall, around this time that I decided to become a doctor. And at the same moment as I began to see a direction for my life and made up my mind, my despondency disappeared. Have you ever experienced something like that?

Honourable Eutychia. I do not tell you this in order to complain about my childhood, but rather to offer you an insight into those things that have formed my life. As an adult I have often thought that the mosaic of the everyday is to be found in the small pieces. And as a doctor I have seen that the experiences of childhood and youth leave their mark upon the fully-grown adult. It is indeed important for your health to dwell upon good memories. What did you like to do as a child? Where was your favourite hiding place? What games did you play? What dreams did you have? Who moulded you when you were growing up? Who did you look up to? How do these people influence you today?

By the way, have you noticed that when we retrieve one happy memory from our lives, others pop up spontaneously? Lately I have asked several of my patients if they can tell me what they rejoice over. The answers are strikingly similar:

When I am absorbed in what I work with.
When I create something.
When I am conscious that I am alive.
When I am aware of the moment.
When I do someone else a favour.
When I make others happy.

The answers reflect two simple truths about joy: Firstly, we experience joy by simply being – by moving a hand or a foot, by breathing, by opening and closing our eyes, by feeling life flow through us. More often however, it is in the very act of making others happy or of creating something, that gives us joy.

Perhaps life itself has its own inherent joy!?

If we just experience it in passing, then short moments can be sufficient to lead to a deep feeling of meaning and gratification. Yes, joie de vivre can be as effective and restorative as medicine.

Experiences of joy help my patients to recover. People who respond positively to the question: "Are you happy to be alive?" find it easier to regain their health than those who answer in the negative.

Honourable Eutychia. Joy is the indomitable sap in every single one of us. Many a life is stretched on a screen filled with sadness. All the same we do not give up, but dare to believe that life has something up its sleeve.

Joy is like a muscle. It needs regular exercise in order to grow.

People believe they can see because they have eyes. But, to probe with the power of sight into the everyday is a talent of the few. Have you, for example, ever experienced living in a certain place, and suddenly – one morning when you are particularly relaxed – you notice a tree you had never seen before, or you become aware of a detail on the front of a house that you had never registered before. It is in this mindful way you discover the everyday with new eyes.

In order to see something, to really see the person you live with or your children or the work you carry out, you need to be alert and take in what you have in front of you. You must dare to be touched by the moment.

> *Joy is everywhere for those of us who still remember to use our eyes and ears as we grow older.*

This gives rise to a warm presence and a generous abundance, moment by moment. Embrace the flowers that spring up from the earth. Rejoice with the birds that fly through the air. Bless the child as it looks up toward the sky and asks in awe and wonder: "Who has put so many stars there?"

Honourable Eutychia. If you allow the source of joy to dry up, it can take a long time to fill your vessels again. Know this:

The joy of life is nurtured through your attention. Its midwife is the small things in your everyday. The language of joy is the language of the senses. Therefore: Eat slowly and really taste the food before you swallow. Love in abundance. Live passionately!

I do not mean to say that you should live in a whirl of pleasure, and give yourself up to self-indulgence. This merely serves to destroy the now and makes you bustled. Attempt rather to grasp the pleasant glimpses that are to be found in everything. Do not let that warm soup get cold while you stretch for a piece of meat. Desist from being vexed about all you lack. It is not necessarily the soup or the piece of meat or the lack of them that your happiness depends on, but that you are capable of receiving and appreciating what you have.

Joy wishes to transform every moment into an inspiring presence. It shows you how you can give to others by making use of your talents and your profusion. Here is a prescription for letting more joy into your everyday.

Prescription for joy

Be generous
Show compassion
Calm down
Enjoy the moment
Begin by seeing the great in the small.

You fill your vessels with joy when you think about and do that which gives you energy, that which arouses your curiosity, that which is of interest to you. Do not ask what you should do.

Explore that which you feel like exploring, that which you haven't tried before, that which is a bit mysterious.

Your mysteries could be extremely everyday-like. What will happen if I stroll down this road instead of taking the usual path? If I light this new incense stick, how will it smell? To change a habit is to throw yourself right into the moment by sharpening your senses.

I remember how particular Grandmother was about creating fine scents in my childhood home. She strew basil and thyme onto the floors. She hung up spice herbs by the bunch in the warmth and where the rays of the sun could reach them in order to release the essential oils. Oftentimes she would sprinkle rosewater upon herself and her surroundings. She dried and cut up plants and roots and made incense to place upon the fireplaces in winter. Pillows were filled with rosemary and placed in the bed so I could bury my nose in it. Dried and salted rose petals were kept in clay pitchers within each room. I remember she removed the lids in the morning so that the pleasant fragrance could waft out and awake me from my slumbering dreams. I yawned and felt enveloped by a good spirit. Grandmother prepared delicious, cosmetic ointments, all types of spiced cough syrups, drinks to fight a fever and balms for cuts and bruises.

Honourable Eutychia. The energy that derives from mindful action is creative. Everything it touches will be renewed. It flows in when you do something that arouses your interest and provides you with the same exultation as when a child flies a kite on a windy spring day.

Mindfulness is the ore of life that waits to be polished and shaped by you. It is not distinct from anything else in your life. Mindfulness is not divided up into moments, levels, quantities or shortcomings. Mindfulness is your attitude towards life – a power to be found whole and intact at all times.

Maybe that is why falling in love is so intense. Romance bursts open the dam of boredom and opens the person to enjoy the stimulating power of mindful attention!

Let me put it this way: On the most profound level you never fall in love by chance. It is Aphrodite who is knocking upon the door of your heart. You become weary of living without passion and you open yourself up yet again to the exuberant juices of the goddess as she comes bursting out of the sea in her shining mother-of-pearl shell, in a carriage drawn by wanton, black seahorses. Can you see her? She stands there naked with her long black hair streaming like a vivacious banner. In the shallows of that person where her seahorses make land, she flings the reins and runs ashore through the sea spray – fired by erotic love. Droplets of salt water fall from her to the earth below and blossom into rose bushes, in every individual she is bid welcome.

Unfortunately, there are many who do not allow themselves to delight or are afraid what the goddess can do to them. I personally have had an ingrained idea that I must not enjoy myself too much, or I will be faced with a corresponding backlash. I have been afraid to submit to the joy of life, because I believed that as great as my joy may be, so would my sorrow rise to match it. As time has gone on, I have searched these thoughts and realized with horror that they impoverish my life. If you are similarly inclined, I can recommend the following. Enter into an agreement with mindful attention every month – where you write a message to yourself and a wish.

Prescription for mindful attention

January:
Mindful attention will help me clear my sight.
Wish: I shall see, hear and feel more attentively every day.

February:
Mindful attention will help me clean away old rubbish.
Wish: I shall rid myself of old habits that are stressful to me, by breathing more attentively every day.

May:
Mindful attention will help me play and laugh more spontaneously.
Wish: I shall honour the moment and count my blessings every day.

Ego sum servus tuus,

Theophilus.

The Magic of the Everyday

is not to dream of a life,

but to live out a dream.

Letter Three

Honourable Eutychia,

Do you play an instrument? Now that I come to think about it, I'm sure you played something for me once. Was it the flute? I hope you still enjoy music, and that the flute isn't lying covered in dust because you do not have anyone to accompany you while you play or because you do not have the time. Do not let your abilities lie fallow! The display of our life is essential to the joy of life. The worth is to be found in the effort, in the challenge, in the process of creation.

If your talents lie dormant, the joy of life suffers. Self-discipline is required for your talents to grow. There is another word for this: strength of character – your ability to motivate and lead yourself, whether it is a question of finishing a piece of work or getting up in the morning. To create a sculpture, paint a picture, draw a building or write a piece of text demands time, discipline and motivation. Without these qualities you will never arrive at a result that you can show to others or delight in yourself. One of the greatest pleasures is to "awaken" after having been absorbed in creative work. Time has stood still. You do not know how long you have been at it. You have been outside of yourself and outside of time, and yet totally present, filled with an intense creative energy.

I myself like to paint. Nothing too ambitious I should mention, but I learned a little from Father when young and I enjoy it tremendously. I need a drawing pin and brushes – some large soft ones and some small firm ones. With rapid strokes I grind colours, filling cup after cup with golden red, sky blue, forest green and sun yellow. At the moment I'm trying to paint a picture of the love of my youth, as I remember her. I hesitate, draw, rub out, and sigh. But I am filled with a strange calmness all the time I work on it, as if I am meditating.

Honourable Eutychia. Sooner or later this question arises at your doorstep: "What kind of life do I want?" You may not utter the question aloud, but you carry it with you. The answer is a vast mosaic of colours with many tiny apportioned pieces. You find a piece here and a piece there. A lot of sky and greenery of course, but also dark valleys and deep waters describe your life's journey. Sometimes you know you have found an important piece that fits into the life you live. Other times you turn a piece around with your head cocked to one side and pout your lips. You pass and ask: "Why did I have to experience this?"

In time, you may discover that it is not only you who ask what the meaning of life is, but that you are also asked: "What have you done with your life? What kind of meaning have you given it?"

Deep down inside all of us there lies a yearning and an idea that we are significant, that we have special talents which will come to expression someday. However, it is all too easy to deceive oneself, to betray what one can become! And when the dreams vanish from life and from work, so does the belief that you can shape your own reality. What dreams did you once hold that you have forgotten or let go of? What kind of dreams do you have now? What are they about? Are you living them? What would happen if you took them out of their hidden places and dusted them off?

As I wrote to you earlier, honourable Eutychia, my life began to drift when my Mother passed away. My Father's life also began to disintegrate. He withdrew into himself and could not bring himself to paint anymore. The family sought counsel from the priest at the Temple of Asclepius. He thought it would be good for Father to get away for a while. "Travel to Athens" was the advice. So Father and I went to Athens. My sister stayed behind with Grandmother. I remember that I looked forward to the trip. As the first spring showers swept in from the sea, Father and I went aboard a Greek ship in the harbour outside Antioch. We sought shelter in the crowded cabin on the afterdeck. Off the western tip of Cyprus we sailed right into a storm. The weather grew more and more inclement. Lightning pierced the night sky in sudden, flashing threads. We were drenched for several days, freezing cold at night and fed upon rusks that were soaked with saltwater. But I was not seasick, and oddly enough, not particularly afraid, even though I was awoken every night by wild dreams. When we finally sailed into the Aegean archipelago, with a good wind and a burning sun, I was excited.

At dawn the next morning I saw the Temple of Poseidon at Cape Sounio hovering like a mirage.

At the magistrate in Piraeus, our documents were scrutinized in silence. The Roman soldiers on guard stood stiff as stone statues and looked out beyond the swarm of people with disinterest. I felt fear creeping up behind me and I noticed that Father bowed down much too far and was friendlier than common courtesy required. "What a fawner," I thought to myself. However, the worst thing was that the feeling stayed with me for a long time afterwards – that father was weak, and that the voyage had been a kind of escape for him. I began to have doubts as to whether he had the necessary strength and know-how to survive in this strange world. At home in Antioch, I had seen Roman troops. They turned up and vanished again like shadows that made life exciting. But here in Athens there were Roman soldiers in every market place and every lane.

We took rooms from a Jewish widow who owned a house on the hill below the Acropolis, not far from the rocky height of Areopagus. Her name was Esther. She reminded me of a bird – thin, alert and serious – yet filled with a strange harmony. I liked to seek her out, listen to what she had to say and savour the smells from the kitchen. She kept a tasty, nourishing table; the kind that makes one's mouth water. Now and again she gave me thirst quenching sweet-

and-sour aniseed to chew upon. The delicate white garlands hung in bundles from hooks in the kitchen roof. After a few weeks she tore the seeds from the stalks, placed them into covered pitchers and used them to make all kinds of biscuits, desserts, sauces and soups. She said that the herb had a rejuvenating effect. That I do not know, but I often recommend pimpinella anisum for the treatment of headaches.

Esther was fond of telling me stories from her religion. I remember listening with bated breath to the story of Joseph who was sold into slavery in Egypt by his jealous brothers when he was seventeen. Think how easy it would have been for him to have lost himself in self-pity, how he could have emphasized his brothers' weaknesses and everything he had lost. But Joseph was too busy thinking about how to make the most of his new situation. Within a short time he had become Potiphar's most trusted servant and oversaw the running of the entire household. He had the full confidence of his master. Then one day Joseph found himself in a difficult situation when Potiphar's wife took a fancy to him. However, Joseph did not succumb to temptation. This made Potiphar's wife so angry that she had him unjustly imprisoned. Joseph had to serve thirteen years in prison for sins he had not committed!

All this time he spent working on his character and in prayer to God. This gave him strength and courage. Soon he was responsible for the running of the entire prison only to end up – after interpreting the Pharaoh's dream – ruling over all of Egypt. He had rank just below the Pharaoh for the rest of his days.

Honourable Eutychia. Here is a prescription for my patients to assist them in getting what they wish for.

Prescription for getting what you want

Take a cup of courage and stir in two spoonfuls of will.
Decide what you want.
Set in motion efforts in that direction.
Make note of what works and what doesn't work.
Don't forget to play. If you stifle, you can easily burn yourself out.
Adjust your approaches.

Remember to celebrate the good results and learn from the bad.

There are times when people come to me and say: "I am sick" or "I am in pain". For those in pain, the suffering overshadows all else. Nobody can deny this. However, I often attempt to get the patients to stop identifying themselves with the illness – as quickly as possible. I bid him or her express it in another way, like: "There is a pain in my head." "My leg, it hurts."

This simple remedy by wordplay often has a healing effect – probably because the patient understands that he or she is much more than the illness.

I have also used this prescription to good effect in other contexts. For example, when you find yourself in the middle of a heated discussion, feel chaos around you and have difficulty seeing the road ahead. Stop for a moment. Avoid identifying yourself with the chaos of emotions. Simply acknowledge this as a fact that lies outside of you. "There is confusion here". Then take a deep breath, plant your feet firmly on the ground and continue the discussion. No one will notice you doing anything out of the ordinary, but you yourself will notice that you become more clear-headed.

Honourable Eutychia. Let me remind you that to attract success is not as simple as thinking the right thoughts, reciting the right prayers, or eating the right food. A little suffering is not always negative for your outcome on the whole. Nor that you must wait a while before reaching your targets. When did you last make a wrong decision? What did you learn from it? What kind of experience did you gain?

Here is some soothing herbal advice to alleviate sorrow and a weak heart: Fennel makes you happy. Sweet almonds fill your mind with new thoughts. Liquorice root aids indigestion and mood swings. And chicken cooked with hyssop cures melancholy – the state of mind that originates from the liver. I have also found that some juice from the mallow plant dissipates sadness and that sage dries it up. Not to mention lemon balm – the very comforter of the heart.

Vale, vale!

Theophilus

The Magic of the Everyday

is not to reach all your targets,
but to mind your steps.

Letter Four

Honourable Eutychia,

Have you breathed today? Ask yourself that question. Or ask a friend. Start by saying: "This question requires a yes or no. When I ask it, answer quickly: Have you breathed today?" Many of my patients answer no to that question, and my own answer often startles me. We breathe, but we are not breathing. We live, but we are not living. We exist, but we are not present in our own lives. We are everywhere, just not here.

I am ashamed to admit it, but I too lack proficiency in this area, and I recognise my own failings in my patients who in their hurried poverty try to act like they have great wealth. Their targets possess them in the same way as if they had a fever.

This is not how my Grandfather was. He had a coffin in his bedroom, which he slept in every Thursday to remind himself that death can strike without warning. Even though Grandmother and the rest of us laughed at his macabre sense of humour, she lined the coffin with red velvet and eider duck and scattered wormwood over him when he lay down to sleep. A strange, slightly scary smell came from the herb-consecrated coffin. I noticed the same smell at breakfast the next morning when Grandfather consumed his morning dram of wormwood wine, while Grandmother hummed and pottered about him.

Wormwood, or artemisia absinthium, is of course one of the doctor's most important servants. However, in order to get more in touch with the moment, I have also developed a few exercises that my patients find most effective. I enclose these with this letter.

Prescriptions for relaxing

When you are tense

When you find yourself in a tense, angry or dejected state of any kind, stop for a moment. Take a good, deep breath. Breathe in slowly through your nose. Fill yourself up completely – and hold your breath for just a moment. Then breathe out.
Breathe in and out like this three times or more.

Now go back to the situation you need to tackle, and you will find that you are in a much better condition to handle it.

Healing drink: Warm goats` milk with camomile.

When you need to wait

When you need to wait, especially when what you are waiting for is unpleasant or you need to carry out something that makes you tense or nervous.

Focus on your breathing. Be mindful of the rhythmic pulse. Notice how you take in air, how you hold it and how you breathe out. Notice in particular that little pause between the three actions – that brief moment where no inhalation or holding of breath or exhalation is taking place. You will soon feel a calm descending upon you.

Healing drink: Hot or cold rosehip juice.

At any time

*Any time you want to refresh yourself
– and also if you are particularly tired,
nervous or tense – try the following:
Open your mouth wide and give a big
yawn as you take a deep breath and stretch
out.*

*This exercise sharpens your mind and
puts you in a better mood right away.*

Healing drink: Boiled water and sage.

Honourable Eutychia. There is not necessarily
some external reason for unpleasant feelings
cropping up again and again in your daily life.
They return because they belong to you. You
created them before you pushed them aside.

Every feeling you experience is your own.

We often make the mistake of thinking we are
frightened, angry or sad because of something
outside of ourselves. In reality, these external
events are triggering factors.

You can only become irritated in areas where you are irritable.

You can only be hurt in areas where you are vulnerable.

Other people act as a mirror for you, so that you may get to know your own reactions better. But neither the person, nor the situation you find yourself in, ever created the feeling. You did it yourself.

You are the creator and the interpreter of your feelings, and ultimately it is you who choose what you will feel.

Let me put it this way: When we allow ourselves to be hurt by other people's behaviour, we often attribute to them the worst intentions – even if that person is a good friend or a loving partner. On the other hand, with regard to our own actions, we do not intend to insult, irritate or denigrate anyone. We are merely absorbed in what is taking place and do not give a great deal of thought as to how it is perceived by others.

If you receive criticism for something you do, I would advise you not to expend all your energy in defending yourself. Rather learn to listen to what your critics say. Let them speak out. Do not interrupt. Ask: "Is that all? Is there anything more?" Assess the motives behind the criticism and be curious as to what you can learn from it.

Honourable Eutychia. The ability to alter perspective is a powerful and effective tool when it comes to tackling negative feelings both in our professional and private lives. A patient told me this story the other day:

A man was advised by his doctor to give money to everyone who insulted him. He was to do this for three years for the sake of his health. When the period of his ordeal was at an end, the doctor said:

"You can journey to Athens now and become wise."

When the man arrived in Athens, he met a wise man who sat by the city gates and offended everyone who went by. That man insulted him, too, but he just broke out in uproarious laughter.

"Why do you laugh when I insult you?" asked the wise man.

"Because for three years I have had to pay for that sort of thing, and now you give it to me for free."

"Enter the city," said the wise man, "it is yours!"

It is my experience that when we run into difficulties, we often take a narrow-minded view of existence. We devote all our attention to worrying about the problem and believe ourselves to be the only ones with such difficulties. This generally leads to a sort of egotism which makes the problem seem even bigger than it is.

When this occurs, it can be helpful to look at things in a wider perspective or from another angle. Instead of pushing the feeling away from you, you can tell it that you will take a closer look. Very often you will find that the emotions are multi-layered.

Anger, for example, has often three causes:

1. *I am afraid*
2. *I am offended*
3. *You or I misunderstand*

Every emotion has a reason to exist, and that reason is always to help you. Feelings are brimming with information. Be curious about what they have to say to you. You do not clarify anything by blocking out your feelings or pretending that they do not exist. Acknowledge and accept that feeling you have right now. Enter into the boredom, displeasure, irritation and disappointment and consider the meaning of what you are experiencing.

Instead of resisting an emotional state, bid it welcome. However, even when you recognise the state you are in, it is by no means certain that you should give vent to it. All too often people confuse being emotional with expressing feelings. This is not the same. You can be good at expressing your feelings without behaving emotionally. And you can be extremely emotional without expressing anything at all.

Honourable Eutychia. I'm trying to get hold of that tender feeling that sits like a painful weight in my body right now. An intense experience of the dark presence of sadness wells up inside me. I wonder what this feeling wants of me, what it is trying to attend to. The answer I am given is surprising. "Be patient." It emerges like the glimpse of a beautiful iridescent pearl below the water. I reflect upon the answer and tie it into my current situation here in Rome. Yes, patience is required of me as I wait to see what will happen to my friend Paul the Apostle.

I weep softly and think of other situations where I have felt a similar sense of sadness. What did I do then? I grab hold of some memories, discover a door ajar and a person listening. Grandmother. The pressure within my body is alleviated at the thought of her. A weight lifts from my brow. The grey colour dissolves and transforms into a hue of red and light green. She serves me a dish of apple slices baked with caraway and some small sweet caraway biscuits. "You must have something sweet to eat," I hear her say in an authoritative voice. "You can't just sit there and mope. Get out into the sunshine and enjoy the taste of the sweet life."

I followed her advice and took a walk outside. I breathed in fresh air and ate some delicious sweet cakes at a bakery in a side street nearby. It relieved my tristesse and unleashed surprisingly an explosive creative energy. Finally I managed to finish the chart that I have been thinking about for a long time – a chart with nine prescriptions to turn negative feelings into positive energy.

How can you convert your negative feelings into positive energy?

Nine prescriptions based on the Socratic Method of Enquiry.

Prescription I

Condition:

> *Uneasiness, often mixed with feelings of indisposition and boredom.*

Cure:

> *You need to find a meaning in what you are doing and in the life you live, or you need to do something else entirely. It is time to deal with questions about yourself and your lifestyle.*

Ask yourself:

> *What are my interests? Am I in the right place? Do I need to begin something completely new? What must change? Where can I be creative? How can I develop some personal new interests? When will I start?*

Prescription II

Condition:

Anxiety, often mixed with worry.

Cure:

Learn to separate what is important from what is really important.
Let go of things you clutch tightly.
Seek inner peace. Meditate every day.
Lift your gaze and accept that you are not in control of everything.

Ask yourself:

Can I share the burden I carry with anyone else? Who can help me?
Are there tasks I need to perform, instructions I would like to give, letters to write? Where and with whom, do I find rest?

Prescription III

Condition:

You feel hurt, often mixed with a feeling of rejection or not being seen.

Cure:

Nurse your wounds for a while by taking a walk in the nature or visiting a friend.

Give your partner or whoever hurt you some time and space.

Breathe with attention many times during the day.

Be kind to animals.

Watch a humorous play at the theatre.

Ask yourself:

How good am I at treating myself to something nice?

How often do I take a bath, soothe my body with fragrant oils or make a nice gesture to myself?

Is there any creative work I can indulge myself with?

Prescription IV

Condition:

Irritation, often mixed with anger.

Cure:

You need to uphold important values in your life that have been trampled on. Draw a line. Tell those around you where your limits are. Stand up for yourself. It is time to find common values with those you are together with.

Ask yourself:

How can I enter into a dialogue with those whom this concerns?

Do I need to prepare arguments and evidence that supports what I want to get across? Which questions need to be discussed? What do we agree upon? What common interests do we have?

Prescription V

Condition:

    Frustration, often mixed with confusion.

Cure:

    You need to get out of your own quagmire. The role of victim does not suit you. Set concrete targets for yourself and follow up with actions.

    Channel your frustration into being creative or start cleaning the room you live in.

Ask yourself:

    What do I want? What is the best thing that can happen now?

    Which plans do I need to set in motion right away?

    Do I dare to put thoughts into action? How and when will I do that?

Prescription VI

Condition:

> Sadness, often mixed with a certain dejection.

Cure:

> Know that you are being trained in patience.
>
> Learn to relax and to trust. Or as my friend Paul says when he quotes the words of Jesus from Nazareth: "Ask, and you shall receive. Seek, and you shall find. Knock and the door shall be opened to you."

Ask yourself:

> When was the last time I laughed?
> What do I need to let go of?
> Do I get enough physical exercise?
> What is my diet like?
> Do I get enough sleep?

Prescription VII

Condition:

Feelings of guilt, often mixed with regret.

Cure:

Humble yourself and be willing to say: "Sorry." Do not wait too long. Be generous. Be loving. It is easy to see the mistakes of another and overlook your own.

Ask yourself:

Whom should I apologize to? And when? How will I behave when the two of us converse?
Will I bring a gift with me?
How can I revive a friendship?

Prescription VIII

Condition:

Inadequacy, often mixed with low self-esteem.

Cure:

You need to take yourself by the hand and develop personally.

Name at least ten of your own positive qualities.

Praise yourself.

It is time to widen your interests and manifest your dreams.

Ask yourself:

Where can I get more knowledge about myself?

Is there anyone who can help me in naming my good qualities?

When do I offer self-encouragement? Once a day?

How do I give myself the recognition I deserve when I accomplish something I set out to do?

Prescription IX

Condition:

Loneliness, often mixed with a feeling of
being outside or different.

Cure:

You need to open up.
You need to show more of an interest in
others.
Come out of your shell and find one or
more friends.

Ask yourself:

How and where can I meet people who
have the same interests as myself?
How good am I at posing active attentive
questions?
Whom shall I visit to get to know them
better?
When will I throw a party?

*H*onourable Eutychia. It did me good to write out these prescriptions.

It has prompted me to believe more in the beautiful thoughts that one must speak of in secret in the little Christian congregation here in Rome. "Look at the lilies in the field. Look at the birds in the air. They do not worry. They are free. Untouched. But God provides for them."

I remember the first time I went to a meeting together with my friend Paul. We entered a large room in the mansion of the Roman woman named Lucina. Slaves and free men and women mingled together. I was surprised that the women seemed so happy and carefree. Many greeted me warmly. An odd naturalness held sway there. The atmosphere was ceremonious, but the service showed more signs of fellowship than of worship. There was talk of taking part in each others' daily lives and helping to shoulder each others' burdens.

Lately we have listened to the words of Mary Magdalene, the women Jesus loved. She is in Rome for a short while, passing through on her way to Gaul. We call her the Apostle of Light. She speaks so beautifully about how we are all capable of performing miracles in our lives and how life with God is about wandering in faith and trust.

"Where God's dream is to be found within you, there lies your treasure," she says.

Ego sum servus tuus.

Theophilus.

The Magic of the Everyday

is not to offer up long prayers,

but to give more thanks.

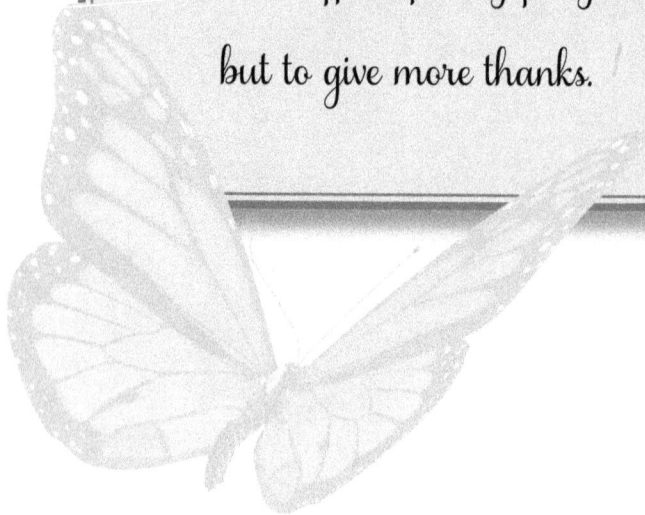

Letter Five

Honourable Eutychia,

Last night I dreamt that I found myself by a mountain crag where I often played as a child. Beneath the crag there was a small hole, but it was overgrown by bushes and thicket. I had to clear my way in order to find the opening. I put my foot down to walk inside, but drew it back quickly with a scream. A partially decomposed body protruded from the ground. A child. A little boy. Despite the contact with the stiff out-stretched hand sending shivers through my whole body, I began to dig at the soil. After that, I lay down beside the dead child, with my cloak over me. I did not know why I did it. I closed my eyes. I lay there for a long time. When my teeth began to chatter, I noticed it was dark. I could not manage to move. The boy looked at me with a hollow glance. Then a pain shot through my body and I awoke.

*H*onourable Eutychia. I have a feeling that the dream has to do with the angst I endure on behalf of my friend's life. It is as if the child in me, the very bearer of hope, is dead. I feel powerless in the situation that Paul now faces – no matter how patient I try to be. In encounters with powerful people, and in particular with the Roman Emperor, everything that is different is killed. That which does not fit into the system must go. Let us kill and have fun!

Panem et circenses. Give the people bread and circuses.

Emperor Nero calls him a political agitator who can set the world on fire. Others upon his council are of the opinion that this man from Tarsus' intention is to shock. They claim that Paul belongs to a group of fanatical Jews who want to awaken a sleeping opinion. Everyone agrees that something suspicious is going on, and that luminous bodies are crossing the night sky. A slave heard flute-like notes whilst he was out seeing to the chickens. A man who was deaf-and-dumb claimed to have been healed.

I am sitting in the darkest corner of the room that I rent here in Rome, as the gladiators enter the arena. I am sitting with my face turned to the window, lonely and confined. The sound of distant shouting can be heard but a few city blocks away. I listen with my back. The endless ring of resounding screams continues monotonously and muffled through the walls.

Quickly I get out of the chair, but remain standing in the middle of the room quivering with indecisiveness. I must save my friend from death, but he is sitting in the gruesome Mamertine prison and there is nothing I can do about it! I hold my head, as if to feel its weight against disastrous decisions.

I hear voices. Three layers of voices. Voices from the past, voices from the present outside in the arena and voices form the future: "Kill him! Kill him!"

Everything is an echo from the dawn of time, and the distant cries become empty in that space they should fill. Hands and feet are ice. My mind is closed. The scream forms, into something that can be hummed with the breath, a prayer: "God, look with mercy upon us poor sinners."

This is how I spend my days and nights now. The nightmare lies just beneath the surface. It is probably only a question of hours before the Apostle is served as carrion to the lions – or perhaps he shall have his head cut off since he is a Roman citizen.

*H*onourable Eutychia. To endure my situation here in Rome, I have lately learned to cooperate with the night when it is tender and close, but also when it is lonesome and frightening, when sleeplessness drains the last remains of the day's strength that I so sorely need.

Sometimes I make myself a soothing drink of valerian root or a dressing of sweet fennel and yarrow, which I place upon my forehead. More often however, I use my therapeutical methods to induce and sustain sleep. I enclose a description of these here:

Prescriptions for sleep

Choose your dream

Lay yourself to sleep in the same way as you would put a small child to bed for the night. There are good curative reasons for the tranquil intimacy by the bedside, the cosy story or the softly sung lullaby. No quarrelling or scolding or unfinished tasks at bedtime. Ask yourself, as you would ask a cherished child: What would you like to dream about tonight? Listen to the answer you give yourself, and say: Yes, now you can sleep and dream that dream.

The languorous lake

Imagine that your mind is a vast, tranquil lake high up in the mountains. You sit down by the shore and open up a piece of cloth you have carried with you. In it lays some precious stones. Take them out now. Hold the stones in your hand; feel their texture and weight, and behold their colour and shape. Then throw them out into the lake, one after another, as you remember a good memory in your life. One stone for each cherished memory. Breathe deeply in and out. Listen to the sound of the first stone as it hits the surface of the water. Look at the ripples that spread out. Enjoy the good feeling.

Count your blessings

Instead of counting you sheep before sleeping, I recommend you to count your blessings. Go through the events of the day, but do so backwards. Start with the last thing you did right before you went to bed. Continue in as much detail as possible and describe to yourself some of the beautiful moments you experienced during the evening and the day. Honour the small things – a song, a smile, a spoken word, a good deed. Most of my patients sleep after counting four to five blessings, and they fall asleep with a light heart.

Evening prayer

Dear God,
Thank you for the day you have given me.
You saw what I did, and what I neglected to do.
You heard what I said and what I did not say, whom I cared about and whom I ignored.
Let all love that was given and received endure.
Let your light that surrounds me, shine through me – more and more.

Amen

Honourable Eutychia. Not too long ago, when Paul was still free to walk about here, we conversed upon my concerns for him in general and for his health and future in particular.

When I close my eyes now, I can see his strong, solid face. He is wearing a worn-out brown cape made of coarse, cheap material. His hands have nails worn down to the quick by work. His eyes lay deep set behind bushy eyebrows. I sense the light that comes from them. We ate a simple meal together that time; freshly baked bread, fresh goat cheese, olives and mild wine. Paul told me not to worry so much, but in all things to let my requests come before God in supplication and prayers of gratitude.

"You should rest, Theophilus," he said, as he gently sighed. "But it is probably as difficult for a doctor as it is for a tent maker."

He continued to talk about how I might under all circumstances, be grateful for everything. I protested and said that I no longer believed in destiny as something inevitable.

"There is a big difference between coming to terms with destiny and giving thanks for everything under all circumstances," he said.

I asked him to be more precise.

"To thank God for everything, also when you meet resistance and rejection, transforms your mind."

"How?"

"You no longer live yourself, but trust lives in you."

"Must I loose myself to learn to trust God?"

He nodded.

"Only that which looses itself, finds itself," he said.

What Paul spoke of that night, has since come to make its mark on the way I live and think. I am a doctor, and rather pragmatic, concerned with what works for the best in our daily lives. Spirituality in my view, can very soon become rather theoretical. However, I have seen lately that trust is as healing as hope – both qualities function as keys to health. One could say with Paul: "Let go and let God."

Honourable Eutychia. Many people imagine that it is hard to trust the dreams that lie within their hearts. The truth is rather the opposite. If you turn away from God's dream in you, it will return to you, again and again during your life. "Thus every good dream is like the grape-vine that Dionysus cultivated," my grandmother said. "When Dionysus was still a small boy, his mother sent him off to Naxos. People were building temples to him there and wanted to worship him as a god when he arrived. Dionysus had to travel on foot. He wandered alone, and the road to Naxos was long. After a while it grew terribly hot and the god boy sat down on a stone to rest. Right in front of his feet there grew a plant which he thought so beautiful that he drew it up by the root in order to take it to Naxos and in time plant it there.

On the way he became worried that the plant would wither in the strong sun. So he put it in a bird claw he found by the side of the road. While he rambled on, the plant began to grow. It wounded its way up and out of the claw so Dionysus had to look for a bigger bone to plant it in. He found a lion's paw by the roadside and that fitted perfectly. But it wasn't long before the plant had outgrown the lion paw as well, and the only thing Dionysus could find now was a donkey paw. He put both the bird claw, and the lion paw into the donkey paw and wandered on.

When Dionysus finally reached Naxos, the plant had grown so much that it twisted around all three animal bones. The god boy put the plant into the ground. He tended to it with care over a long time and the plant grew steadily lush. Eventually it yielded an abundance of fruit – in the form of beautiful bunches of grapes. It was the grapevine Dionysus had discovered along-side the road and which he had refined by his divine touch," said Grandmother. "Afterwards he crushed the grapes into the loveliest wine and gave it to people when they came to worship him and pay homage. And so it is that when people drink the wine which Dionysus offers them, they first become as light as birds, then as brave as lions, only to end up as foolish as donkeys. They leave their dreams strewn along the side of the road, and are unable to remember them when they awake."

Honourable Eutychia. Life is generous in its support, but people often have difficulty in accepting that which is offered to them. Some of the gifts we receive, we scarcely look at before we hand them back with the excuse that they are of no use or that we are too afraid of failure. There are very few of us who really dare to do what is necessary in order to cultivate our dreams so that they can grow from deep down in our hearts and bear fruit in our daily lives.

Most of us live in a world where we are used to categorizing phenomena as warm or cold, good or bad, light or dark, right or wrong. We attempt to divide up what is happening into either-or and we see things in black or white. The mindful key seldom springs from an either-or attitude. On the contrary, it reveals itself through a range of paradoxes, something which involves a both-and perspective:

The first paradox you run into is that nothing in life is predestined while at the same time nothing is random or happens by chance either.

The second paradox is that you have free will, yet you are not in control. You can make plans, but circumstances can conspire to hold them in check. What you do about it is up to you. Sometimes you have a wealth of choices. Other times it seems you arrive at an impasse. Nevertheless, the history is alive with tales of people who have suffered under the most extreme conditions and displayed both ordinary and extraordinary courage, compassion and creativity – like my friend Paul.

The third paradox is that you experience pain, even though you trust in that the Goddess of Love is working for you and wants only the best for you.

*H*onourable Eutychia. Pain has taught me to be aware of the moment and to take notice of the now. In times of sorrow, when the future is too painful to think about, and the past too difficult to remember, I have learnt to become aware of the light that is found in the small details. Every moment bears with it a safe stone to rest your head upon. 'Every moment, taken alone, you can manage to endure,' I tell myself. 'A deal fell to pieces yesterday. Your dear friend can die tomorrow. But right now, right at this moment, you are here, looking out over the tumultuous sea. You breathe in and out. You have a warm cloak around you. Dare to believe that every moment carries with it its own grace.' Or as Mary Magdalene says: "Fear not the unknown, for every man can grasp that which they want and need."

To offer thanks for everything under all conditions, even though pain is present, is a matter of deep trust.

I have come to believe that within every person there is a quiet room with an altar and healing water to be found. When we knock at that door and go inside, we immediately notice that peace descends and the heart is becalmed. If we do not enter the room, we will constantly be divided in our decisions, stressed by all the outside voices and wishes and all the expectations and opinions we meet during our everyday.

*H*onourable Eutychia. For someone who has spent time in the desert, as I have, this insight no longer appears odd. Maybe I wanted to realize an old boyhood dream the first time I journeyed into that vast, stony infinitum. I wanted to follow in Joseph's footsteps to Egypt, as Esther had described to me, and travel with a caravan of spice traders. There were approximately two hundred people and twice as many animals. I had bought a camel, but I struggled to mount it. When I finally succeeded, we were already on the move. I did not exchange many words with anyone to begin with, but instead sat in silence and watched the animals and people journey through this strange landscape.

"I have crossed this desert many times," a camel driver said to me one night, as we sat and ate dates by the campfire. "The desert is so big, and the horizon so far away, that people feel small and hold their tongues."

We started moving in the morning, stopped when the sun was at its hottest and continued in the afternoon. We were always mindful of the wind. Sometimes the desert was of sand, other times of stone. When the caravan came to a stony section, it went around, and the detour was even longer when we came upon large rocks. But no matter how many detours we had to take, it struck me that the caravan always continued toward the same point. As soon as the obstacles were overcome, we followed the star that guided us once more. When we saw it twinkle in the sky, we knew that it was leading us to water, dates and palm trees.

I became friends with the camel driver who often rode alongside me. We told each other stories when we sat around the fire at night. I remember he said to me that the life of a camel driver is about being able to read the signs in the ever shifting sands, and to live in trust.

Something of the same is implied by my friend Paul the Apostle. I shall attempt to repeat what he said to me word for word, as I remember it from our last conversation some time ago. "To give thanks does not mean that you accept the current situation as something unalterable and final," he said. "Thanksgiving is of all things the very counterbalance against the current state. Through the prayer of thanksgiving you come into God's peace, Theophilus. Subsequently, it's a matter of not losing that peace whether at work or play. Trust is the dominant attitude that you practice during meditation and which you later carry with you out into your daily activities."

He leaned across the table and whispered:

"Your only important task is to rest in God under all conditions. That's when something important happens. You move from a thinking prayer of the words to a listening prayer of the heart. To pray and meditate does not mean to hear yourself speak, but to be quiet until you sense the presence of God. You do not enter this silence in order to withdraw, but in order to come closer – to yourself. Taste a little silence every day, and your moments will be full of wonder."

Prescriptions for training your silence

The rose

> Find a place in your home or in the nature
> where you can be alone.
> Sit down. Relax. Breathe.
> Focus on a rose that you have put in front
> of you.
> Look at the beauty of the flower. Admire
> the form. Be attentive to the smell. Sense
> the feeling that it stirs within you.
> Smile.
> Do this every morning if possible.

The cat

> Find a place where there is a cat, a cow,
> a dog or a bird – at least an animal that
> you like.
> Sit down close to it. Relax. Breathe.
> Watch the animal. Look at it as it walks
> or sleeps or licks itself.
> Give it some good thoughts.
> Enjoy the silent relationship between you.
> Do this once a week.

The void sky

Find a place where you can be by yourself.
Sit down. Breathe. Close your eyes.
Watch your thoughts come and go. Let them pass.
Try not to hold unto any memory, feeling or future worry.
If you grasp yourself in doing so, then stop as soon as you become aware of the attachment. Blank it out by focusing on your breath.
Breathe in and out.
Do this once a day especially in the afternoon.

Honourable Eutychia. That is how I remember Paul spoke to me. The last night we spent together became a turning point in my life. When I left him later that night, I felt that the stars had a hold on me like they had previously revealed themselves to me in the desert. I focused my attention on the stars above me, and what my friend had just told me – until I realized that I stumbled around like a drunkard. I stopped and took a deep breath.

A little boy ran past me, barefoot, clutching an apple. A mule driver stood by the fountain further on and let the fresh water run into his hands – which he used as a bowl. After he had stilled his thirst, he rubbed his wet hands over his face, muttered thanks, picked up an empty melon peel, filled it up with water and carried it over to the animal so that it also might drink.

I closed my eyes and opened them again – slowly. I sensed that this night I had leaned against a profound insight that I had never known before. I felt that I was beginning an apprenticeship in order to develop a new, mindful heart.

Servus tuus nunciam, vale.

Theophilus

The Magic of the Everyday

is not to be busy,

but to be present.

Note upon origin of the letters

By Professor of Archaeology Torgny Sodergren, University of Uppsala, Sweden.

To my darling wife,

The manuscript you are now holding in your hands is a copy of an ancient papyrus roll written in Greek mixed with some Latin words and expressions which I personally have deciphered and translated. The papyrus roll was probably found together with a quantity of other writings by an Egyptian farmer called Muhammad Ali al-Samman near the town of Nag Hammadi, one December day in 1945. This is how it came about:

A few days before they were to carry out a vendetta for the murder of their father, Muhammad Ali and his brothers rode out on their camels to dig for sabakh – a fertile earth which they usually scattered upon the fields. Whilst they dug around a large elevation, they came across a red, earth-like pot. Muhammad Ali was hesitant to smash it to pieces, as he was sure it hid an evil spirit. But since it was also possible it could conceal old gold coins, he couldn't stop himself. It turned out to contain thirteen papyrus books, all bound in leather.

When the brothers came home to al-Qasr that night, Muhammad-Ali dumped the books nonchalantly in front of the fireplace where his mother was about to cook some food. He used part of the papyrus sheets to light the fire with. But a few weeks later, whilst the police were nosing around the cabin investigating the blood feud the brothers were involved in, Muhammad Ali grew fearful that they would discover the ancient books and punish him. Thus he asked the village priest to hide some of them. At the same time a local history teacher managed to get his hands on one of the papyrus rolls and immediately sent it to a friend in Cairo in order to get it valued.

A black market process without parallel was underway. The rolls were sold in bits and pieces to eager antique dealers in Cairo and collectors from all across the world went to Egypt in order to buy whatever they could come across. A colleague of mine, Professor Gilles Ouispel in the Netherlands, asked the just renowned Jung Institute in Zurich to buy one of the bound book rolls. They succeeded in this. To my tremendous surprise we deciphered the text and I could read the following:

"These are the secret words that the living Jesus did say and which his twin, Judas Thomas wrote down."

What we held in our hands was a hitherto completely unknown gospel, namely the gospel according to Thomas, which is probably the oldest gospel to exist. Bound in the same book was the gospel according to Philip, a similarly hitherto completely unknown text, which describes more thoroughly Jesus' relationship with Mary Magdalene:

"Jesus loved her more than the other disciples and often used to kiss her upon the mouth."

It soon became apparent to us that we were in possession of ancient secret texts of great value written about AD 50 – or a short time before the other four gospels which are contained within the New Testament. These secret writings were probably concealed within the clay pot by a Coptic monk around AD 300, so as to avoid them being burnt during the Church's intensive attempts to destroy all so-called heresies.

Upon closer perusal, my colleague and I discovered that some pages had been torn out. I went to Egypt, in the spring of 1952, in order to try and locate these in the Coptic museum. Several of the rolls that had been confiscated by the Egyptian government had been placed there. I was met with the utmost scepticism; one might even term it disdain. It dawned on me that the competition between different researchers, collectors, antique dealers and archaeologists on who could get their hands on the scrolls and study them was in full swing. I couldn't even gain admittance to view the scrolls, and my time in Cairo was in the process of turning into one long nightmare.

Just before I was due to return to Sweden, I had a visit from Albert Eid, a Belgian antique dealer residing in Cairo. In all secrecy, he showed to me scrolls he claimed had come from the same find at Nag Hammadi. I eventually bought these for a large sum and smuggled them with me out of the country. In light of the treatment I'd received, I was not particularly disposed towards the Egyptian authorities and decided to try to engage UNESCO to take up the fight with the Coptic museum in order to make copies of the scrolls available to the public. As you're aware, it took many years before my colleagues and I succeeded in this. But in 1972, the first photographic representations of the texts were available, and the remainder of the copies are in the process of being released now.

I therefore ask of you, my darling wife, that these ancient letters you hold in your hand be published – when you feel the time is right. The original scroll lies hidden at the Jung Institute in Zurich. Whilst I translated and deciphered it, I found that it contained letters and prescriptions written by a doctor named Theophilus to a woman by the name of Eutychia. It's not known who this woman was. Perhaps she was a scholar or maybe just a figment of the doctor's imagination. It was not unheard of, at that time, for scholars to write letters with a certain ethical or moral message to a fictional character, instead of writing a textbook. A Greek physician of the time would also have a full command of Latin, which was the official language. For the sake of curiosity, I have let some of the Latin words remain in the translated text.

No matter who this woman was in relation to this doctor called Theophilus at the time he wrote the letters, for me you will always be my own darling Eutychia – friend of joy.

Yours,
Torgny

The Magic of the Everyday

is not to travel far away, but to find your
  way home

is not to own more, but to allow more in

is not to dream of a life, but to live out
  a dream

is not to reach all your targets, but to
  mind your steps

is not to offer up long prayers, but to give
  more thanks

is not to be busy, but to be present.

Arctic Queen

Arctic Queen

The Pearl

A poetic story about finding your talents
and using them

Dignity Press
WORLD DIGNITY UNIVERSITY PRESS

ISBN 978-1-937570-00-2

"What a magnificent story. Wonderfully emotional
and irresistibly readable."
Kvinner og Klær

"Narrative art at its best,
packed into a pocket-sized format."
Morgenbladet

"A rare pearl – heartfelt and simple in all its depth."
Ellen Arnstad, chief editor, Henne

You may find interest also in these
Dignity Press books:

Ada Aharoni
Rare Flower
Life, Love, and Peace Poems
ISBN 978-1-937570-10-1

Francisco Cardoso Gomes de Matos
Dignity – A Multidimensional View
Rhymed Reflections
ISBN 978-1-937570-37-8

Mark Tarver
Conversations of Taoist Master Fu Hsiang
About Love, Evil, and Human Nature
ISBN 978-1-937570-52-1

George W. Wolfe
Meditations on Mystery
Science, Paradox and
Contemplative Spirituality
ISBN 978-1-937570-49-1

Visit www.dignitypress.org to see the
complete program of Dignity Press and
World Dignity University Press

www.ingramcontent.com/pod-product-compliance
Lightning Source LLC
Chambersburg PA
CBHW031437270326
41930CB00007B/750